THERE'S A SAYING FOR THAT

Proverbs from Around the World

EDITED BY BOB BLAISDELL

DOVER PUBLICATIONS, INC.
MINEOLA, NEW YORK

Bibliographical Note

There's A Saying for That: Proverbs from Around the World is a new work,
first published by Dover Publications, Inc., in 2013.

International Standard Book Number
ISBN-13: 978-0-486-49074-8
ISBN-10: 0-486-49074-2

TEXT DESIGN BY PAULA GOLDSTEIN, BLUE BUNGALOW DESIGN

Manufactured in the United States by Courier Corporation
49074201
www.doverpublications.com

NOTE

Three characteristics has a proverb: few words, right sense, fine images.
—from the Arabic

Proverbs are like backward jokes. We hear the punchline and imagine a situation. My favorite collection of proverbs, Paul Rosenzweig's *The Book of Proverbs: Maxims from East and West*, is arranged by nation, but I decided I liked the idea of sorting proverbs by topic. Then I discovered that this type of arrangement made nonsense of the categories. Is the American proverb "Every dog has his day" really about *dogs,* or the Latin "Man is wolf to man" about *wolves*? I don't think so. Then what about the many dictionaries of proverbs arranged alphabetically? That system struck me as a stuttering of non sequiturs: "A fish . . . A fool . . . A fowl . . . A fulsome . . ." I came to agree with Hanan J. Ayalti, the editor of *Yiddish Proverbs,* who declared, "Any attempt at dividing the material itself into logical groups would have interfered with the very nature of the proverb, which resists consequence and subordination." So, Rosenzweig's random assortment by nation won out after all. I have arranged the proverbs not to build on or play off of each other, but to encourage a continual refocusing—to induce a pause for thought. "I always imagine for myself a series of stories—pictures—illustrating the proverbs," Lev Tolstoy wrote in 1862. At the school he set up for peasant children, the great Russian writer taught lessons on proverbs, using them as inspiration for some of his own masterful short stories and as themes for beginning writers.

Built into national, regional, and linguistic categorization is the difficulty or *impossibility* of tracing a proverb's nationality; proverbs hop like fleas and thus travel well. "The heart that loves is always young," says a Canadian proverb; it could have originated anywhere on earth. After some fussing about each proverb's national origin, I began to feel that translation into English makes all the proverbs foster children of English. When it was not possible to label a proverb by nation, I identified it by language or source (e.g. Yiddish, Swahili, Latin, Arabic, the Bible, or a people, e.g.,

Bambara, Masai). China has many languages; the proverbs that are labeled as "Chinese" I have simply assigned to China.

Good proverbs make us feel smart but not superior; we recognize that if a proverb points out a fault, we as fellow-travelers on the Ship of Fools share a claim in it. There's a lot of weight and refinement to folk wisdom, which has been milled and processed by many hundreds of years and countless *experiences*. It's hard not to see that such everyday wisdom suggests that people are people, and have been wrestling with their souls for a long, long time. The feelings and actions of selfishness and kindness, desire and resignation, acceptance and frustration, and love and grief have been around forever, and they'll be around "A hundred years hence," when "we shall all be bald," as the Spanish proverb goes.

If a proverb doesn't explain itself to you, give a shrug and let it go, but all of the ones I've chosen I selected because they began spinning stories in my imagination. Another Spanish proverb, "Half-way is twelve miles when you have fourteen miles to go," reminds me of the difficulty of finishing off a half-marathon in Brooklyn or a 900-word introduction to a book I love. If a proverb needed a gloss, it missed the boat and we have sailed without it. On the other hand, for clarity's sake, I have tweaked phrasing in a handful or two of the translations from Russian and Spanish. Similarly, I have carried over most of the Scottish expressions into conversational English. For instance, "*A gude tale is no' the waur o' bein' twice tauld*" has slid into "A good tale is none the worse for being twice told."

Besides, as far as Western languages go, Rosenzweig says: "The end of the growth of proverbs in Europe is usually judged to be in the later Middle Ages." So if our great-grandparents wouldn't have said it or heard it, it's probably not in here. I am grateful to the scholars of proverbs whose books I have learned and borrowed from, among them Wolfgang Mieder. If I have misattributed the nationality of any proverb, I apologize: "God send me a friend that may tell me my faults; if not, an enemy, and he will."

—Bob Blaisdell
NEW YORK CITY
JUNE 2012

There's a Saying for That

CONTENTS

AFRICA

BAMBARA

One here-it-is is better than ten you'll-get-it-laters.

BUGANDA

The one who talks thinks, but the one who does not talk thinks more.

The one who goes to see his mushrooms every day can pick them when they are ripe.

CONGO

Everyone is polite to a chief, but a man of manners is polite to everyone.

There's a Saying for That

To love someone who does not love you
is like shaking a tree to make the dew drops fall.

Man is like palm wine: when young, sweet,
but without strength; when old, strong and harsh.

Every bird thinks its nest is the best.

We all love money, but money loves only some of us.

 DAMA

The wise man will not say what you did wrong until
you ask him.

A man may be famous in the world and yet small
in his own house.

A child with parents remains a child.
An orphan will soon be an adult.

 EGYPT

If you see a town worshiping a calf, mow grass and feed him.

Even a blind cat will still want to hunt mice.

A thousand cranes in the air are not worth one sparrow in the fist.

Obey your tongue and regret it.

 ETHIOPIA

If you work like a slave you will eat like a king.

There's a Saying for That

He who conceals his disease cannot expect to be cured.

The eye has never seen enough, the ear has never
heard enough.

The body is earth. When earthenware breaks,
it reverts to earth.

 EWE

The well brought up man eats with one hand even when
he is hungry.

The Hare says: "Walking slowly leads to death."
The Chameleon says: "Walking quickly leads to death."

 GANDA

He that sets only one trap will not eat meat.

 GHANA

When your child pretends to be dying,
then you pretend to be making preparations
for his funeral.

 GUINEA

A thought, once written down, does not get lost.

We cannot love that which we do not know.

There's a Saying for That

 **KENYA**

If the baboon could see his own behind,
he would laugh too.

 **KIKUYU**

Frowning frogs cannot stop the cows drinking
from the pool.

 **KIMBUNDU**

Death shakes us off like the wind shakes the leaves
from the trees.

Man is looking for wealth while Death is looking
for him.

 KUNAMA

They say there is a God, but He is often asleep.

 LIBERIA

No man will starve in his mother's house.

 MADAGASCAR

Who knows what hurts himself
knows what hurts others.

A good wife is easy to find, but suitable in-laws are rare.

Seeking redress in court is like putting your hand
in a hornet's nest.

 **MALI**

A lonely truth can be brought down by a pack of lies.

Your son is always better than your brother's son.

 **MASAI**

A dispute between brothers does not have to be settled
by the chief.

 **MOROCCO**

One day you will have to beg God for mercy.
Be merciful to beggars now.

An old woman can outwit even the devil.

 NAMIBIA

You cannot escape God.
You will meet Him in foreign lands.

Smiling teeth are like an empty ostrich egg.

 NANDE

After the worms have eaten your father
they will eat you.

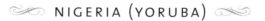 NIGERIA (YORUBA)

When truth is missing, proverbs are used to discover it.

A woman who has not lived with two husbands
will never know which is the better.

Truth cannot be sold on the market place,
but lies are bought with ready cash.

If you will never offer palm wine to your uncle,
you will not know many proverbs.

You don't divorce someone who rides horses
and then marry someone who walks on foot.

Frowning and fierceness
do not prove manliness.

Eyes never see a beautiful woman without greeting her.

A wise man who knows proverbs reconciles difficulties.

Even the sharpest knife-blade
cannot carve its own handle.

A man does not run among thorns for nothing;
either he is chasing a snake or a snake is chasing him.

Proverbs are horses for solving problems.

 NIGERIA

Hand and tongue never give alike.

The handsome man is king, if there is no rich man near.

There's a Saying for That

When the mouse laughs at the cat
there is a hole nearby.

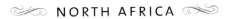

Two strong men will move a heavy stone.
Two bright lawyers will not agree about the
meaning of a word.

A handful of luck is better than a donkey-load of learning.

Your chief and your wife: let them talk first.

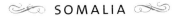 SOMALIA

The word that leaves your mouth leaves your control.

 SOUTH AFRICA

If you learn it while young, you can do it when old.

Each man for himself and God for all of us.

Old goats love young green leaves.

A blind man may hear more than you see.

Modesty shows good upbringing,
but without it you will be richer.

 SWAHILI

Do not try to fight a lion if you are not one yourself.

A man's knowledge cannot be read in his face,
nor can a woman's virtue.

There's a Saying for That

We are all beggars at God's door.

Where there is smoke, there is fire. Where there is fire there
are people. Where there are people there are also
wicked people.

If the trunk dies, the branches die too.

If God wishes a man to go astray,
He will make his heart blind.

Learning is like sailing the ocean: no one has ever seen it all.

You cannot turn the wind, so turn your sail.

Love is like an illness and the loved one is the only medicine.

The seeker of drunkenness will one day have enough.
The seeker of knowledge will never have enough.

A letter from the heart can be read on the face.

When you see sailboats sailing,
remember how hard it was to build them.

You cannot bring back love or life.

Courage is the fruit of the decision in the heart.

Does the mosquito thank you for your blood?

Without children a house is sad and silent.

Even God has patience with people.

There's a Saying for That

 **TETELA**

You hide your faults behind a wall,
but you parade your neighbor's faults in the market.

 **UGANDA**

People will never agree, but rain will make them all
run for shelter.

"No more trouble," you say
when the one you love arrives.

 **WEST AFRICA (ASHANTI)**

The tongue kills a man and the tongue saves a man.

WEST AFRICA (FULFULDE)

Lying will get you a wife but not keep her.

WEST AFRICA

The parasite has no roots.

Until the lions produce their own historian,
the story of the hunt will glorify only the hunter.

YAUNDE

Do not propose to a girl whose home you have not seen.

 ZAIRE

DEMOCRATIC REPUBLIC OF CONGO

If you don't like the frog because it eats slugs,
then you will have no meal.

The man in love is blind.
The woman in love has her eyes half open.

 ZANDE

God gave us the seed of every plant,
but we must sow it.

 ZIGULA

Old age is like weeds: they come slowly but will one day
cover the whole field.

ZIMBABWE

The axe forgets, but the tree cannot forget.

If you can walk you can dance, if you can talk you can sing.

ZULU

You have to ask your friend to help you put the load
of firewood on your back.

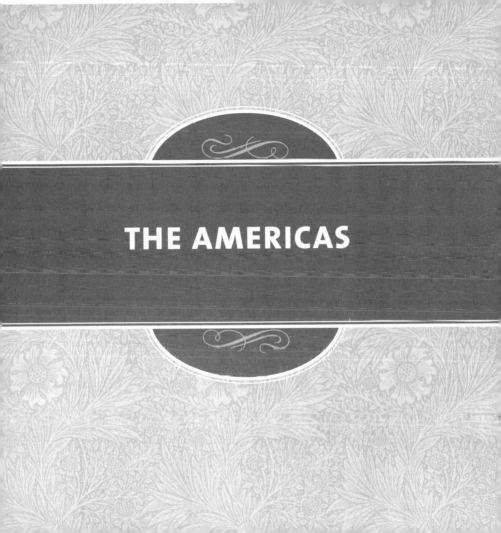

THE AMERICAS

ARAPAHO, NORTH AMERICA

Before eating, always take a little time to thank the food.

ARGENTINA

He who has bad habits loses them late or never.

He who has no malice fears no malice.

BLACKFOOT, NORTH AMERICA

Life is as the flash of the firefly in the night,
the breath of the buffalo in winter time.

 **BRAZIL**

Haste is the mother of imperfection.

Goods that are much on show lose their color.

Love is blind but marriage restores one's vision.

Where blood has been spilt, the tree of forgetfulness
cannot flourish.

 **CANADA**

The heart that loves is always young.

The devil places a pillow for a drunken man
to fall upon.

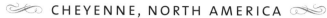 CHEYENNE, NORTH AMERICA

Judge not by the eye but by the heart.

Beware of the man who does not talk,
and the dog who does not bark.

Do not judge your neighbor
until you have walked two moons in his moccasins.

 CREE, NORTH AMERICA

When the last tree is cut down, the last fish eaten
and the last stream poisoned, you will realize
that you cannot eat money.

 CROW, NORTH AMERICA

Old age is not as honorable as death,
but most people want it.

 ECUADOR

The devil is wiser more because of his age than on account
of being the devil.

The idle remarks of the rich are taken as maxims
of wisdom by the poor.

A silk dress doesn't mean clean undergarments.

What you deserve, you don't have to ask for.

A mirror doesn't know how to lie.

I would rather be deceived by an intelligent person
than by a jackass.

Arriving and leaving, hoping and remembering,
that's what life consists of.

God has only one measure for all people.

No matter how beautiful the shoes are,
they still have to go on the ground.

 HONDURAS

Every time one laughs, a nail is removed
from one's coffin.

IROQUOIS, NORTH AMERICA

Remember your children are not your own
but are lent to you by the Creator.

The words of God are not like the oak leaf,
which dies and falls to the earth,
but like the pine tree,
which stays green forever.

Plantain ripe, can't green again.

A cockroach never so drunk him walk a fowl yard.

Keep both eyes open before you are married,
and afterwards close only one.

If man can't dance, him say de music no good.

De higher monkey climb, de more him expose.

 LAKOTA, NORTH AMERICA

The frog does not drink up the pond in which he lives.

Sometimes dreams are wiser than waking.

 MEXICO

God gives the rich money, because if they didn't have it
they would starve to death.

Love is blind—but not the neighbors.

"Here we are," said the fly to the ox upon which it sat,
"plowing this field!"

You have to learn how to love
before you learn how to play.

Ambition never has its fill.

With patience and spit, an elephant can even
pick up an ant.

When in doubt, consult your pillow.

Better to die on your feet than to live on your knees.

The sun is the blanket of the poor.

Marriage is the only war where you sleep with the enemy.

You sing of heartbreak when you cannot cry.

Everyone makes firewood of the fallen tree.

A busy ant does more than a snoozing ox.

Trust your best friend as you would your worst enemy.

An ounce of joy is worth more than an ounce of gold.

Even if the cage is gold, it's still prison.

When young, illusions; when old, reminiscences.

He who lives with hope dies happy.

The throat must pay for what the tongue may say.

Of doctor, poet, musician and madman,
we each have a trace.

The lazy one works twice as much.

Time heals and then it kills

It is not enough for a man to know how to ride;
he must also know how to fall.

Do good and don't care to whom.

 NAVAJO, NORTH AMERICA

Always assume your guest is tired, cold and hungry,
and act accordingly.

 OMAHA, NORTH AMERICA

The lazy man is apt to be envious.

Ask questions from the heart and you will be answered
from the heart.

 PERU

Only he who carries it knows how much the cross weighs.

Youth is intoxication without wine;
old age, wine without intoxication.

From the tree of silence hangs
the fruit of tranquility.

Fortune and olives are alike: sometimes a man has
an abundance and other times not any.

PUEBLO, NORTH AMERICA

Cherish youth, but trust old age.

Men in search of a myth will usually find one.

PUERTO RICO

She who desires to see desires also to be seen.

We like the treason but not the traitor.

When the devil prays, he wishes to deceive you.

The evil that issues from your mouth
falls into your bosom.

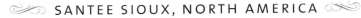

SANTEE SIOUX, NORTH AMERICA

A child believes that only the action of someone who
is unfriendly can cause pain.

SENECA, NORTH AMERICA

Every fire is the same size when it starts.

Even in paradise, living all alone would be hell.

UNITED STATES

Never trouble trouble till trouble troubles you.

God helps the poor, the rich help themselves.

When all you have is a hammer,
everything looks like a nail.

An expert is one who knows more and more
about less and less.

Half the trouble in this world comes from saying "Yes"
too quick and "No" not soon enough.

Never give a sucker an even break.

If it ain't broke, don't fix it.

There's a Saying for That

People give nothing so willingly as advice.

Even the devil was an angel in the beginning.

You can't know a girl by her looks
nor a man by his books.

Every dog has his day.

Mule don't kick according to no rule.

If you want something done, ask a busy person.

Truth is the first casualty of war.

A woman convinced against her will
is of the same opinion still.

You can't tell a book by its cover.

The rich get richer and the poor get babies.

Even the devil will swear on a stack of Bibles.

Business is business.

Good clothes open all doors.

He that marries for money will earn it.

Hope is a good breakfast but a poor supper.

There's always room at the top.

Any publicity is good publicity.

There's a Saying for That

Nothing is certain in this world but death and taxes.

There is no fool like an old fool.

A thief believes everybody steals.

Nothing so bad but it might have been worse.

Better an old man's darling than a young man's slave.

The Lord prefers the common people;
that's why he made so many of us.

Silence gives consent.

Love me, love my dog.

When one door shuts, another opens.

Many hands make light work.

Envy is the sincerest form of flattery.

The female of the species is more deadly than the male.

If you want to lead, you must be able to follow.

There are three faithful friends—
an old wife, an old dog, and ready money.

Forbidden fruit is sweetest.

There's a Saying for That

Don't tell tales out of school.

Marry a handsome man
and you marry trouble.

History is fiction with the truth left out.

Better a dollar earned than inherited.

When drink enters, wisdom departs.

Necessity is the mother of invention.

He that plants trees loves others besides himself.

Learning makes a good man better
and a bad man worse.

Love laughs at locksmiths.

Every man judges others by himself.

If you sing before breakfast, you'll cry before night.

No news is good news.

A true friend never offends.

Truth is the opinion that survives.

The tree is no sooner down than everyone runs
for his hatchet.

The best patch is of the same cloth.

Them as has, gits.

There's a Saying for That

You can't take it with you.

When poverty comes in at the door,
love flies out at the window.

Better an hour too early than a minute too late.

Ask me no questions, I'll tell you no lies.

True lovers are shy when people are by.

Once doesn't count.

Nothing dries sooner than a tear.

Choose your love, then love your choice.

What cannot be cured must be endured.

Many a child is hungry because the saloon-keeper is rich.

The only secret a woman can keep is that of her age.

The sight of lovers feeds those in love.

A handful of knowledge is worth
a bushelful of learning.

A woman always thinks it takes two
to keep a secret.

Every light has its shadow.

It is not enough to aim, you must hit.

The blow that liberates the slave sets the master free.

The busiest men have the most leisure.

Many things are lost for want of asking.

Don't tell all you know nor do all you can.

You can't put thanks in your pocket.

It is better to love someone you cannot have
than have someone you cannot love.

It is better to be a has-been than a never-was.

One murder makes a villain, millions a hero.

If you can't be good, be careful.

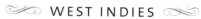

The jay bird don't rob his own nest.

When the goat's foot is broken,
then he finds his master's door.

ANCIENT TONGUES
AND TRADITIONS

ANCIENT GREEK

A library is a repository of medicine for the mind.

Act quickly, think slowly.

A miser is ever in want.

God delays but does not forget.

He who has learned unlearns with difficulty.

Every liar has another for his witness.

Man has many projects, but God cuts them short.

Don't hear one and judge two.

There's a Saying for That

Against stupidity, the gods themselves
fight unvictorious.

Call no man happy until he dies.

Second thoughts are best.

If the doctor cures, the sun sees it;
but if he kills, the earth hides it.

Sleep is the brother of death.

Gain does not delight as much as loss grieves.

Marriage is the only war that men pray for.

Seize the end and you will hold the middle.

The submitting to one wrong brings on another.

The net of the sleeper catches fish.

The gods sell all things to hard labor.

 BABYLONIAN

The gods do not deduct from man's allotted span
the hours spent in fishing.

A living dog is better than a dead lion.
ECCLESIASTES 9:4

As you sow, so you reap. Be not deceived;
God is not mocked: for whatsoever a man soweth,
that shall he also reap.
GALATIANS 6:7

The tongue can no man tame: it is an unruly evil,
full of deadly poison.
JAMES 3:8

Every tree is known by his own fruit.
LUKE 6:44

Judge not, that ye be not judged.
MATTHEW 7:1

The spirit indeed is willing, but the flesh is weak.
MATTHEW 26:41

Pride goeth before destruction, and a haughty spirit
before a fall.
PROVERBS 16:18

It is better to dwell in the wilderness than with
a contentious and angry woman.
PROVERBS 21:19

As cold waters to a thirsty soul,
so is good news from a far country.
PROVERBS 25:25

A flattering mouth worketh ruin.
PROVERBS 26:28

He that maketh haste to be rich shall not be innocent.
PROVERBS 28:20

There's a Saying for That

HEBREW

Love is a sweet dream
and marriage is the alarm clock.

He is not called wise who knows good and ill,
but he who can recognize of two evils the lesser.

Pride is the mask of one's own faults.

The sun will set without thy assistance.

A lie stands upon one leg, truth upon two.

The soldiers fight and the kings are heroes.

Teach the tongue to say, "I do not know."

 THE KORAN

There is a devil in every berry of the grape.

 LATIN

Better be first in a village than second at Rome.

No one is so old that he does not think he could live another year.

Small sorrows speak; great ones are silent.

The remembrance of past sorrows is joyful.

Night is the mother of counsel.

What one knows is sometimes useful to forget.

Where there's life there's hope.

Submit to the rule you have yourself laid down.

Promises must not fill the place of gifts.

Whatever precepts you give, be short.

Soon ripe, soon rotten.

Patience abused becomes fury.

In avoiding that which is evil
I have found that which is good.

Small favors conciliate, but great gifts make enemies.

Hard by the river, the fool digs a well.

A flattering speech is a honeyed poison.

Fashion is more powerful than any tyrant.

Beware of the man of one book.

He that cannot obey cannot command.

He sends his presents with a hook attached.

Where there is honey, there are bees.

Self-praise is no recommendation.

Today, you; tomorrow, me.

The fool binds a dog with the gut of a lamb.

A man should be religious but not superstitious.

There's a Saying for That

All ask if a man be rich, none if he be good.

By doing nothing we learn to do ill.

The more laws, the more offenders.

Even a hare will insult a dead lion.

He who does not love does not strive.

Pretense of love is worse than hatred.

You can drive out Nature with a pitchfork,
but she keeps on coming back.

Familiarity breeds contempt.

Man is wolf to man.

Virtue is its own reward.

Where there is love, there is faith.

 TALMUD

Two coins in a bag make more noise than a hundred.

Thy friend has a friend, and thy friend's friend
has a friend; be discreet.

THE BRITISH ISLES

ENGLAND

Whatever man has done, man may do.

The real dread of man is not the devil but old age.

There's never a new fashion but it's old.

Truth needs no memory.

Gratefulness is the poor man's payment.

He who loves you well makes you weep,
and he who hates you may make you laugh.

He who is shipwrecked a second time cannot lay
the blame on Neptune.

There's a Saying for That

Every man has his price.

Some go to church to see and be seen, some go there to say
they have been, some go there to sleep and nod,
but few go there to worship God.

Deeds are fruits, words are leaves.

Nature takes as much pains in the forming of a tree
as she does an emperor.

Truth may be blamed but shall never be shamed.

Little wit in the head makes much work
for the feet.

Truth will sometimes break out unlooked for.

Every man thinks his own geese swans.

Virtues all agree, but vices fight one another.

Wine is a turncoat, first a friend and then an enemy.

The rich man has his ice in the summer and the poor man
gets his in the winter.

Of money, wit and wisdom, believe one-fourth
of what you hear.

Wisdom don't always speak in Greek and Latin.

Youth and white paper take any impression.

Evil is sooner believed than good.

There's a Saying for That

There are a thousand hacking at the branches of evil
to one who is striking at the root.

The fox may grow gray but never good.

Young men think old men are fools, but old men
know young men are fools.

Old sins cast long shadows.

It is easier to pull down than to build up.

If there were no receivers there would be no thieves.

If you can't ride two horses at once, you shouldn't
be in the circus.

Youth looks forward but age looks back.

A good painter can draw a devil as well as an angel.

He that would go to sea for pleasure,
would go to hell for a pastime.

Everyone speaks well of the bridge
which carries him over.

It is not spring until you can plant your foot
upon twelve daisies.

Three may keep a secret, if two of them are dead.

It is an Englishman's privilege to grumble.

Pictures are the books of the unlearned.

Talk of the devil, and he is bound to appear.

You cannot make people honest by an
Act of Parliament.

Life is short and time is swift.

Love needs no teaching.

God sends good luck and God sends bad.

Little strokes fell great oaks.

Hear twice before you speak once.

The devil tempts all, but the idle man tempts the devil.

To travel through the world, it is necessary to have the mouth of a hog, the legs of a stag, the eyes of a falcon, the ears of an ass, the shoulders of a camel, and the face of an ape, and, overplus, a satchel full of money and patience.

Never try to prove what nobody doubts.

In war, all suffer defeat, even the victors.

Abroad one has a hundred eyes, at home not one.

War is sweet to them who know it not.

There's a Saying for That

Every man has the defects of his qualities.

Whatever is made by the hand of man,
by the hand of man may be overturned.

Knowledge makes one laugh,
but wealth makes one dance.

The love of money and the love of learning
rarely meet.

From hearing comes wisdom;
from speaking, repentance.

The wise seek wisdom, a fool has found it.

Who is not ready today will not be ready tomorrow.

The bread never falls but on its buttered side.

You must look where it is not, as well as where it is.

Men make houses, women make homes.

The pen is the tongue of the hand.

A wise man changes his mind, a fool never.

A well-bred dog goes out when he sees them preparing
to kick him out.

The master has still one trick more than he teaches.

She loves the poor well, but cannot abide beggars.

Many a man's tongue has broken his nose.

The cock crows, but the hen lays the eggs.

Where God has his church,
the devil will have his chapel.

Things not possessed are always best,
but when possessed are like the rest.

Send a wise man on an errand, and say nothing to him.

Striving to do better, oft we mar what's well.

Put your finger in the fire
and say it was your fortune.

Who proves too much proves nothing.

In overmuch disputation the truth is lost.

Bad weather is always worse through a window.

Excess of obligation may lose a friend.

A fault confessed is half redressed.

There goes more to marriage than four bare legs
in a bed.

Money, like manure, does no good till it is spread.

In vain the net is spread in the sight of the bird.

"Had I known" was a fool.

After your fling, watch for the sting.

To do great work, a man must be very idle
as well as very industrious.

There's a Saying for That

Call on God, but row away from the rocks.

Getting out of doors is the worst part of the journey.

Fingers were made before forks.

The same fire that melts the butter hardens the egg.

Believe nothing of what you hear
and only half of what you see.

The best is the enemy of the good.

Old praise dies unless you feed it.

The bleating of the kid excites the tiger.

God is a good worker, but he loves to be helped.

God send me a friend that may tell me my faults;
if not, an enemy, and he will.

Speak me fair and think what you will.

A wise man will neither speak nor do whatever anger
would provoke him to.

None is a fool always, everyone sometimes.

He who seeks trouble never misses it.

Flee the pleasure that will bite tomorrow.

Better suffer a great evil than do a little one.

Neither praise nor dispraise yourself,
your actions serve the turn.

There's a Saying for That

Rats and conquerors must expect
no mercy in misfortune.

A good maxim is never out of season.

He who once hits will be ever shooting.

The least foolish is accounted wise.

Life is half spent before we know
what it is to live.

He that cannot speak well of his trade
does not understand it.

If things were to be done twice, all would be wise.

Every ass thinks himself worthy to stand
with the king's horses.

Use soft words and hard arguments.

He who will be his own teacher often has a fool
for his student.

When sorrow is asleep, wake it not.

All complain of want of memory,
none of their judgment.

A friend's frown is better than a fool's smile.

If the best man's faults were written on his forehead,
it would make him pull his hat over his eyes.

A man may be great by chance, but never wise
or good without taking pains for it.

Success makes a fool seem wise.

A man never has too much honesty.

Forget others' faults by remembering your own.

He has but sorry food that feeds upon
the faults of others.

They who seek only for faults see nothing else

'Tis easier to avoid a fault than acquire perfection.

That is not good language which all understand not.

He who will not be counseled cannot be helped.

Words instruct, but examples persuade effectually.

Faults are thick when love is thin.

Go not to hell for company.

It is not work that kills, but worry.

Walnuts and pears you plant for your heirs.

The best books are those which the reader thinks he could
have written himself.

Two in distress make sorrow less.

Desire of glory is the last garment that even wise men put off.

A good surgeon must have an eagle's eye,
a lion's heart and a lady's hand.

One may say too much even upon the best subject.

Some that speak no ill of any, do no good to any.

It is wit to pick a lock and steal a horse, but wisdom
to let it alone.

When a stone leaves the hand, it belongs to the devil.

If thou be a stranger be merry and give the first good-morrow.

Success is by acting, not wishing.

A thief passes for a gentleman when stealing has made him rich.

Fools tie knots and wise men loosen them.

God deliver me from a man of one book.

Never joke with stupid people.

Too much breaks the bag.

There's a Saying for That

He looks one way and rows another.

Be slow in choosing, but slower in changing.

He that will not sail until he have a full, fair wind
will lose many a voyage.

A man should not stick his nose in his neighbor's pot.

Solomon made a book of proverbs, but a book of proverbs
never made a Solomon.

Mingle a little folly with your wisdom.

 IRELAND

It's almost as good as bringing good news not to bring bad.

Where the tongue slips, it speaks the truth.

If you have to give advice to lovers, find out what they want
first and advise them to do that.

Give away all you like but keep your bills and your temper.

It is not easy to steal where the landlord is a thief.

Borrowing borrows sorrowing.

A new broom sweeps clean, but the old brush
knows the corners.

Never give cherries to pigs nor advice to a fool.

To a wedding wait to be invited;
to a funeral go uninvited.

There's a Saying for That

If a mother has no beauty in her face she has it in her heart.

Never trust a fine day in winter,
the life of an old man or the word of an important
person unless it's in writing.

Don't throw away the dirty water until you are sure
you have clean water.

If my father had made me a hatter,
men would have been born without heads.

On the Irish ladder of success
there's always someone on the rung above
using your head to steady himself.

It's hard to choose between two blind goats.

Better an ass that carries you
than a fine horse that throws you.

Hating a man doesn't hurt him half as much as ignoring him.

Good manners are often better than good looks.

Don't bless with the tip of your tongue
if there's bile at the butt.

No property—no friends; no rearing—no manners;
no health—no hope.

If you're the only one that knows you're afraid, you're brave.

A clever crook dresses well.

A verbal agreement is not worth the paper it's written on.

Hold on to the bone and the dog will follow you.

The loneliest man is the man who is lonely in a crowd.

Death is the poor man's physician.

I want his company as much as a headache wants noise.

Sneering does not become either the human face
or the human soul.

Even if you are on the right track,
you'll get run over if you just stay there.

Enough is as good as plenty.

Death looks the old in the face and lurks behind youth.

A scholar's ink lasts longer than a martyr's blood.

There are more lies told in a wake-room than
in a court-room.

A drink is shorter than a good yarn about it.

The schoolhouse bell sounds bitter in youth
and sweet in age.

Be happy with what you have and you'll have plenty
to be happy about.

He'd step over ten naked women to get at a pint.

A man that's fond of reading
will never finish tidying his loft.

There's a Saying for That

Learning is a light burden.

The best way to get rid of your enemies is God's way,
by loving them.

The family that has no skeleton in a cupboard
has buried it instead.

A man in need of a drink thinks of wiser schemes
than the great generals of our time.

Better the coldness of a friend
than the sweetness of an enemy.

An old broom knows the dirty corners best.

Experience is a hard school, but a fool will learn
in no other way.

An old dog sleeps near the fire
but he'll not burn himself.

Bricks and mortar make a house
but the laughter of children makes a home.

A family is never as close as when it's in mourning.

The apple will fall on the head that's under it.

There's no war as bitter as a war between friends.

What brings death to one brings life to another.

If a man is his own ruin let him not blame fate.

If we fought temptation the way we fight each other
we'd be a nation of saints again.

There's a Saying for That

Two persons never lit a fire without disagreeing.

God gave us two ears and one mouth
and we should use them in the same proportions.

Work never killed a man, but play
is often the best medicine.

It's harder to become honest than it is to become rich.

If you haven't been taught by God
you'll not be taught by man.

The elbow on the bar-counter points the way to Hell.

Hope is the lazy man's spade.

There's nothing so bad that it could not be worse.

You don't have to live with the man you cheat,
but you have to live with your conscience.

Those who make the laws
are often their greatest breakers.

Greatness in a man knows modesty.

A man works hard for success and then squanders his time
talking about it.

Marriage changes a man and makes the woman
that changed him whine about his not being
the same man she married at all.

Patience is like love: you must have it
to know about it.

There's a Saying for That

A politician is a man who can find a problem
in every solution.

It's better to like what you do than to do what you like.

If you say everything you want to say,
you'll hear something you don't want to hear.

A kind word never got a man into trouble.

Speak neither well nor ill of yourself.

The busy man is the man who makes time to help.

If you'd prefer to be doing something else,
you're working.

A questioning man is halfway to being wise.

Work for one thing and you'll gain another.

You won't be able to tell how much money a man is earning
by looking at his clothes,
but you will by looking at his wife's.

Every invalid is a physician.

The clever man discovers things about himself
and says them about others.

A charitable man has never gone to Hell.

There's a Saying for That

SCOTLAND

A bald head is soon shaven.

Better your feet slip than your tongue.

A bold foe is better than a cowardly friend.

A fool is happier thinking well of himself
than a wise man is of others thinking well of him.

A gnarled tree may bear good fruit,
and a harsh nature may give good counsel.

There's none so busy as him that has least to do.

A good tale is none the worse for being twice told.

Danger past, God forgotten.

A thread will tie an honest man
better than a rope will do a rogue.

Better speak boldly out than always be grumbling.

Old saws speak truth.

A wise man wavers; a fool is fixed.

Children speak in the field
what they hear in the house.

When drink's in, wit's out.

Women and wine, dice and deceit,
make wealth small and want great.

Better deaf than hear ill tales of oneself.

Years bring fears.

Birth's good but breeding's better.

Do nothing in a hurry but catching fleas.

Daylight will peep through a small hole.

When a lady lets a fart, the dog gets the blame.

Better be envied than pitied.

Don't lift me before I fall.

You cannot take clean water out of a foul well.

Do a man a good turn, and he'll never forgive you.

Better be the head of the commons than
the tail of the gentry.

Drink little, that you may drink long.

Better live in hope than die in despair.

Drunken joy brings sober sorrow.

There's a Saying for That

Words are but wind, but seeing's believing.

Bees that have honey in their mouths
have stings in their tails.

Don't sigh for him, but send for him;
if he be unhanged, he'll come.

You have a head, and so has a nail.

Empty barrels make the most din.

Use of hand is father of knowledge.

Better lose your joke than lose your friend.

Don't tie a knot with your tongue that you can't loosen
with your teeth.

Were it not for hope the heart would break.

What never climbs never falls.

You cannot put an old head upon young shoulders.

You'll live long after you're laughed at.

God help the poor,
for the rich can help themselves.

 **WALES**

Do good and then do it again.

No man is good unless others
are made better by him.

Faults are thick where love is thin.

Deep lies the heart's language.

He who is blameless is not yet born.

The best economy, economy of words.

Determination is a good horse.

King Arthur could not tame a woman's tongue.

A wolf's teeth may be removed,
but not his nature.

Money is the key that opens all locks.

Let not your tongue cut your throat.

A good aunt is a second mother.

It is easier to say "mountain" than to climb one.

He who desires to be praised, let him die.

The guilty one will flee without being pursued.

Speak well of your friend;
of your enemy say nothing.

Love your neighbor but maintain your hedge.

A job started is two parts done.

One gets the truth from the simple.

A word to the wise, a stick to the unwise.

What is done by night will be seen by day.

Jealousy does not grow old.

Enough is a little more than you already have.

Man's best candle is his understanding.

If every fool wore a crown,
we should all be kings.

To love a woman who scorns you is to lick honey from a thorn.

Grief will sleep but anxiety will not.

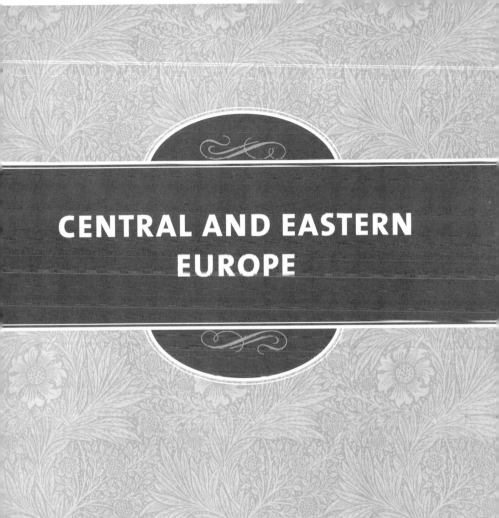

CENTRAL AND EASTERN EUROPE

BOSNIA

Day by day passes until the last stands behind the door.

BULGARIA

A tree falls the way it leans.

CZECH REPUBLIC

Many a friend was lost through a joke, but none was ever gained so.

Love is a disease, but it does not want to be healed.

Many doctors, death accomplished.

 ## ESTONIA

Love makes cottages manors; straw, silken ribbons.

He that is worth anything is talked about.

A son is a son until he takes a wife.

 ## FINLAND

Age does not give sense, it only makes one go slowly.

 ## GYPSY/ROMANI

Good horses can't be of a bad color.

When you are given, eat; when you are beaten, run away.

In selling a horse praise his bad points,
and leave the good ones to look after themselves.

Too often the courage about dying is cowardice
about living.

As long as there are some poorer than you,
praise God even if you are unshod.

God bless your legs for bringing you here.

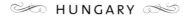 HUNGARY

The wise man, if he stumbles, falls heavily.

Outside Hungary there is no life; if there is any,
it is not the same.

A crow does not louse the buffalo to clean him
but to feed himself.

Love, smoke, and coughing cannot be hidden.

A flatterer is a secret enemy.

Illness gives us the taste for health.

 LATVIA

The hidden stone finds the plough.

You lift it, I'll do the groaning!

If the fool have a hump no one notices;
if the wise man have a pimple everybody talks about it.

 MONTENEGRO

Where there is least heart there is most speech.

Advice is like medicine; the better it is, the nastier to taste.

 POLAND

One man may teach another to speak, but none can teach
another to hold his peace.

Love enters a man through his eyes,
woman through her ears.

One beggar does not hate another as much as
one doctor hates another.

Choose your wife by your ear rather
than by your eye.

Ask the patient, not the physician, where the pain is.

 ROMANIA

A bag full of flour and a purse full of money
are the best relations in the world.

If you wish to die young, make your physician your heir.

A prudent man procures in summer the sleigh
and in winter the wagon.

 **SERBIA**

A foolish fox is caught by one leg, but a wise one by all four.

 **SLOVAKIA**

A secret love is always a true love.

 **SLOVENIA**

The threshold is the tallest mountain.

 **UKRAINE**

An old woman without her mate
is like borscht without bread.

There's a Saying for That

He who loves with his heart finds the words to say it.

Lovers always find a place to meet.

If the heart is not in it the words will fool no one.

 YIDDISH

When the heart is full, the eyes overflow.

When you have a pretty wife, you are a bad friend.

Not the mouse is the thief, but the hole in the wall.

Where there is love, it never feels crowded.

A man should live if only to satisfy his curiosity.

A deaf man heard a mute tell how a blind man
saw a cripple run.

When a fool holds his tongue, he too is thought clever.

"Rejoice not at thine enemy's fall"—
but don't pick him up either.

The wise man, even when he holds his tongue,
says more than the fool when he speaks.

Don't judge a man by the words of his mother,
listen to the comments of his neighbors.

Husband and wife are one flesh, but they possess
two separate pockets.

A mother understands what a child does not say.

There's a Saying for That

A pretty face costs money.

All things grow with time, except grief.

If only man were as worthy of help as God is able
to provide it.

A man's worst enemy can't wish him what he thinks up
for himself.

What good is the cow that gives plenty of milk
and then kicks over the pail?

A man is not honest simply because he never had a chance to steal.

Before you marry, make sure you know whom you are going to divorce.

It is better for my enemy to see good in me than for me to see evil in him.

Truth is the safest lie.

Love is sweet, but it tastes best with bread.

Between husband and wife only God is a judge.

It's never too late to die or get married.

Half a truth is a whole lie.

There's a Saying for That

A wise man hears one word and understands two.

A job is fine but interferes with your time.

Man is stronger than iron and weaker than a fly.

Mix with your neighbors, and you learn
what's doing in your own house.

With money in your pocket, you are wise
and you are handsome
and you sing well, too.

A man is what he is, not what he used to be.

The poor man has few enemies, the rich man fewer friends.

God hands out punishment, man takes revenge.

Reason is a slowpoke.

The cat likes fish but hates to wet her paws.

Heaven and hell can be had in this world.

From fortune to misfortune is but a step;
from misfortune to fortune is a long way.

God loves the poor and helps the rich.

What's straight to your face is slander behind your back.

Ten lands are sooner known than one man.

There's a Saying for That

You must not tell a lie,
but you're not bound to tell the truth.

If the rich could hire others to die for them,
the poor could make a nice living.

As you look at a man, so he appears.

Parents can provide a dowry, but not good luck.

Many complain of their looks, but none of their brains.

If charity cost no money and benevolence caused
no heartache, the world would be full of philanthropists.

Too humble is half proud.

Two things are a burden: a fool among wise men
and a wise man among fools.

Where the wife is queen, the husband is king.

Wanting to be wiser than all is the greatest folly.

Let a fool throw a stone into a well and ten wise men
can't get it up again.

We know the time of our setting out,
but not of our return.

Ever since dying came in fashion, life hasn't been safe.

Ten lands are sooner known than one man.

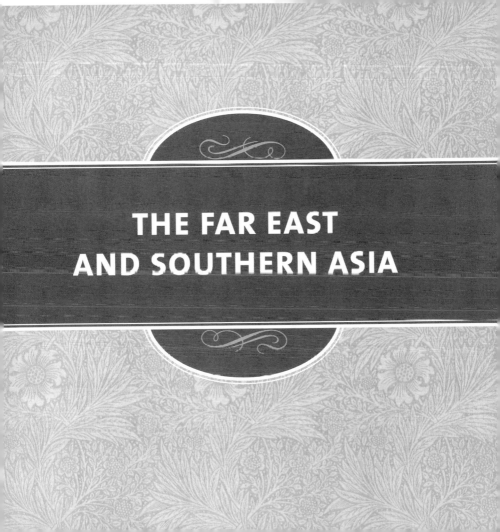

THE FAR EAST
AND SOUTHERN ASIA

CHINA

Patience is a tree with bitter roots that bears sweet fruits.

With money you are a dragon, with no money a worm.

When a finger points at the moon, the imbecile looks
at the finger.

Pioneers plant trees but the latecomers rest in the shade.

Words are mere bubbles of water,
but deeds are drops of gold.

A general's triumph means ten thousand rotting bones.

Sin is the root of sorrow.

There's a Saying for That

Preserve the old but know the new.

Great generals need not blow their own trumpets.

It may cost a million to buy a house, but ten million to find
good neighbors.

It's easier to make a feast than to get the guests to come, and
it's easier to get guests to come than to
entertain them properly.

Often give, often receive.

Experience is a comb which nature gives us
when we are bald.

Misfortune is not that which can be avoided,
but that which cannot.

Do not remove a fly from your friend's forehead
with a hatchet.

Men trip not on mountains; they trip on molehills.

A man without a smiling face must not open shop.

When a man is angry, he cannot be in the right.

When you go to buy, don't show your silver.

Love your children in your heart, but be stern with them
in your manner.

Not all who are bitten by dogs are thieves.

To spoil what is good by unreasonableness is like
letting off fireworks in the rain.

When two partners are of one mind,
clay is into gold refined.

He who strikes first admits that his ideas have given out.

He who rides the tiger can never dismount.

Half a truth engenders a new lie.

Princes do not think of rendering their subjects happy unless
they have nothing else to do.

Riches only adorn the house,
but virtue adorns the person.

You cannot prevent the birds of sadness from flying over your head, but you can prevent them from nesting in your hair.

He that is afraid to shake the dice will never throw a six.

Drunkenness does not produce faults, it discovers them.

The tongue which is yielding endures, the teeth which are stubborn perish.

To persecute the unfortunate is like throwing stones on one fallen into a well.

A single conversation across the table with a wise man is better than ten years' study of books.

If you ferry people, ferry them to the opposite bank;
if you build a pagoda, build it up to the top.

Truth often hides in an ugly pool.

One hundred careful plannings cannot avoid one slip.

Something is learned each time a book is opened.

The local ginger is not considered spicy.

The father in extolling his son extols himself.

The best cure for drunkenness is while sober
to see a drunken man.

He who praises me on all occasions
is a fool who despises me
or a knave who wishes to cheat me.

Whether or not a dumpling is decently filled with meat
cannot be judged from how well the decorative folds
are made on the outside.

Empty words are scattered in all directions by the wind,
but proverbs learned by heart are fixed in the mind.

To believe in dreams is to spend all one's life asleep.

Just as a fast horse needs only one touch of the whip,
so a straightforward person needs only a word
in order to understand or make a decision.

Who is the greatest liar? Who talks most of himself.

If you don't scale the mountain you can't view the plain.

The only equal treatment in the world is white hair.

It is easier to know how to do a thing than to do it.

It is not the anger of the father but his silence
that the well-born son dreads.

One day of life is worth more than
a thousand years of death.

By nature all men are alike, but by education
widely different.

If you long for pleasure, you must labor hard to get it.

Accumulation of money is as slow as picking up soil
with a needle.

A wind as big as a bushel can get through a hole
as small as the point of a needle.

Never be boastful; someone may pass who knew you
as a child.

If you stay with bricklayers for three nights,
you may not learn how to build houses,
but at least you'll learn how to carry bricks.

Seek friends who are better than you, not your own kind.

Everything is difficult at first.

If you would not be cheated, ask the price at three shops.

Pull one hair and the whole body moves.

A clever man turns great troubles into little ones
and little ones into none at all.

Be correct yourself, before you correct others.

Some people do not blame the shortness of their own rope
but rather blame the deepness of the old well.

Keep company with good men
and good men you'll imitate.

You had better return home and make a net than go down to
the river and desire to get fish.

Other people's flatulence stinks, but one's own is fragrant.

Forethought is easy, repentance hard.

If you want your dinner, don't offend the cook.

A man must make himself despicable
before he is despised by others.

A diamond with a flaw is preferable to a common stone
without any imperfections.

With patience the mulberry leaf becomes a silk gown.

To see a man do a good deed is to forget all his faults.

One dog looks at something, and a hundred dogs at him.

He who insults me to my face can yet be an honest man
and my friend.

There's a Saying for That

Believing all books is worse than believing none.

Kindness is more binding than a loan.

Riches come better after poverty than poverty after riches.

A day of sorrow is longer than a month of joy.

The gem cannot be polished without friction
nor man perfected without trials.

Dig a well before you are thirsty.

True friendship is clear, like water.
False friendship is sweet, like honey.

He who asks is a fool for five minutes.
But he who does not ask remains a fool forever.

Without clouds, there can be no rain.

To bow the body is easy, to bow the will is hard.

Married couples who love each other tell each other
a thousand things without talking.

A man thinks he knows, but a woman knows better.

A truly great man never puts away
the simplicity of a child.

There's a Saying for That

With happiness comes intelligence to the heart.

One joy scatters a hundred griefs.

Failure is the mother of success.

When you aim at the rat, beware of the vase.

Although there exist many thousand subjects for elegant conversation, there are persons who cannot meet a cripple without talking about feet.

Lending is like throwing away; being paid back is like finding something.

Who knows himself knows others.

Master easy, servant slack.

The first time a girl marries, she consults her parents' wishes;
the second time, her own.

The rich man thinks of the future,
the poor man thinks of today.

Heaven and hell are within the heart.

Slander cannot make a good man bad;
when the water recedes the stone is still there.

Vast chasms can be filled, but the heart of man never.

To give without cause is to bribe.

No man ever became thoroughly bad all at once.

There is no economy in going to bed early to save candles
if the result be twins.

There's a Saying for That

One man will carry two buckets of water for his own use;
two men will carry one for their joint use;
three men will carry none for anybody's use.

To open a shop is easy, to keep it open an art.

Don't rejoice over him who goes
before you see him who comes.

Do not forget little kindnesses, and do not remember
small faults.

Every book must be chewed to get out its juice.

INDIA (BENGALI)

Sweet mouths gain heart's wishes.

The sieve says to the needle, "You have a hole in your tail."

INDIA (HINDI)

The happy wife is she whose husband
asks no questions.

The love of a foreigner
warms like a bonfire of loose grass.

Silence never makes mistakes.

There's a Saying for That

INDIA (MARATHI)

She who has one child cries,
she who has two cries, she who has seven cries,
and she who has none . . . she also cries.

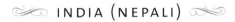

INDIA (NEPALI)

Only money in your hand and your wife in sight
belong to you.

INDIA (PUNJABI)

Does love have a religion?

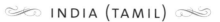

Can you mature fruit by beating it with a stick
when it does not ripen of itself?

The goddess of misfortune dwells in the feet
of the sluggard.

A weeping man and a smiling woman
are not to be trusted.

A prudent youth is superior to a stupid old man.

The rock that resists a crow-bar gives way to the roots
of a tender plant.

Silence puts an end to quarrels.

 INDIA

Anger ends in cruelty.

Do not blame God for having created the tiger,
but thank him for not having given it wings.

 INDONESIA

The turtle lays thousands of eggs without anyone knowing,
but when the hen lays an egg
the whole country is informed.

He that can see a louse as far away as China
is unconscious of an elephant on his nose.

Although it may rain, cast not away the watering pot.

The betrothed of good is evil, the betrothed of life is death,
the betrothed of love is divorce.

 JAPAN

The frog in the well knows nothing of the sea.

Fall down seven times, get up eight.

A man in love mistakes a harelip for a dimple.

If I peddle salt, it rains; if I peddle flour, the wind blows.

Women and sparrows twitter in company.

Feed a dog for three days and he will remember your
kindness for three years; feed a cat for three years and she
will forget your kindness in three days.

A sorrow is an itching place that is made worse
by scratching.

Proof rather than argument.

The absent get farther off every day.

There is more delight in hope than in enjoyment.

A statement once let loose cannot be
caught by four horses.

Wine is the best broom for troubles.

Forgiving the unrepentant
is like making pictures on water.

What has been the fashion will come into fashion again.

 TIBET

Men may look alike but their hearts differ.

FRANCE

A lie travels round the world while truth is putting her boots on.

If youth only knew! If age only could!

I know by mine own pot how others boil.

One may go a long way after one is tired.

Try to reason about love and you will lose your reason.

Go back a little to leap the further.

In all things man's choice is not between the good and the bad, but between the bad and the worse.

Love makes time pass; time makes love pass.

There's a Saying for That

The stable wears out the horse more than the road.

When we cannot get what we love, we must love
what is within our reach.

Love never dies of starvation
but often of indigestion.

The surest way to remain poor
is to be an honest man.

A love defined is a love that is finished.

Cats, like man, are flatterers.

Young men forgive, old men never.

Being loved is the best way of being useful.

Adversity makes men, prosperity monsters.

He who can lick can bite.

He who disparages wants to buy.

A clear conscience is a good pillow.

Vows made in storms are forgotten in calms.

He who is near the church is often far from God.

It is a stupid goose that listens to the fox preach.

It is an old cow's notion that she never was a calf.

What is learned in the cradle lasts to the grave.

Mother's love is ever in its spring.

A man is not to be known till he takes a wife.

None are so busy as those who do nothing.

Laughter does not prove a mind at ease.

The guilt and not the scaffold makes the shame.

Patience is the only universal medicine.

Justifying a fault doubles it.

God alone understands fools.

The Germans carry their wit in their fingers.

It is more disgraceful to suspect our friends
than to be deceived by them.

A woman's tongue is her sword
and she does not let it rust.

One must lose a minnow to catch a salmon.

Take a woman's first advice, not her second.

Love, your pains are worth more than
all other pleasures combined.

Don't find fault with what you don't understand.

There's a Saying for That

From the sublime to the ridiculous is only a step.

It is better to have to do with God than with his saints.

'Tis the wisest thing in the world to be a good man.

That is a good sorrow which makes a man
the better for it.

If men were cured of their silly fancies,
they would have little pleasure left.

The wisest man would be counted a fool
if we could see all his thoughts.

When glory comes, memory departs.

God saves the moon from the wolves.

"Perhaps" hinders folks from lying.

Men judge of things more frequently
by the prejudice they have got
than by their own knowledge.

Poverty is no sin.

He who wants to be rich in a year
comes to the gallows in half a year.

"They say" is a fool or a liar.

Love brings the distant near.

A woman and a melon are hard to choose.

A stingy man is always poor.

Dress slowly when you are in a hurry.

All the treasures of the earth would not bring back
one lost moment.

A brain is worth little without a tongue.

One never goes so far as when one doesn't know
whither one is going.

There is not enough if there is not too much.

Fortune can take from us
only what she has given us.

Gentleness does more than violence.

A guest and a fish after three days are poison.

He who is judge between two friends
loses one of them.

Labor rids us of three great evils:
tediousness, vice, and poverty.

The law says what the king pleases.

Life is half spent before one knows what life is.

Love makes time pass away,
and time makes love pass away.

Misfortunes come on horseback and go away on foot.

Praise the sea and keep on land.

He who has his purse full preaches to the poor man.

Who is in the right fears, who is in the wrong hopes.

A sack was never so full
but it could hold another grain.

It is only at the tree loaded with fruit that people
throw stones.

People count up the faults of those
who keep them waiting.

When there is marriage without love, there will be love
without marriage.

There's a Saying for That

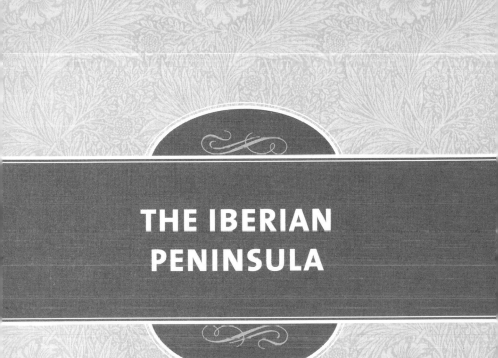

THE IBERIAN
PENINSULA

PORTUGAL

Love is like the moon: if it doesn't get bigger,
it gets smaller.

The wolf loses his teeth but not his inclination.

Lay your hand on your bosom and you will not speak ill
of another.

Where the river is deepest it makes least noise.

Rather go rob with good men than pray with bad.

A poor man is hungry after eating.

More grows in a garden than a gardener sows there.

Never cut what can be untied.

The fool who is silent passes for wise.

What is bought is cheaper than a gift.

 SPAIN

Since you can bear with your own,
bear with other men's failings too.

There is no more faithful nor pleasant friend
than a good book.

Punishment is a cripple, but it arrives.

Lovers swear that everyone else is blind.

When love is not madness, it is not love.

Never advise a man to go to war nor to marry.

The wrath of brothers is the wrath of devils.

No man is quick enough to enjoy life to the full.

He that marries a widow will often have a dead man's head
thrown into the dish.

Tomorrow is often the busiest day of the week.

In love all is sadness; but sadness and all,
it's still the best thing in life.

It is not in the pilot's power to prevent the wind
from blowing.

There's a Saying for That

A boy's love is water in a sieve.

God keep you from "It is too late."

I suspect that ill in others which I know by myself.

He who resolves to amend has God on his side.

If you would be Pope, you must think of nothing else.

I wept when I was born, and every day shows why.

In war, hunting and love, you have a thousand sorrows
for every joy or pleasure.

Let nothing frighten you but sin.

I am no river but can go back
when there is reason for it.

A cheerful look and forgiveness is the best revenge
for an affront.

The spider's web lets the rat escape
and catches the fly.

One love drives out another.

Since you know everything, and I know nothing,
pray tell me what I dreamed this morning.

There's a Saying for That

The father's virtue is the best inheritance a child can have.

No sensual pleasure ever lasted so much as for a whole hour.

Never deceive your physician, your confessor,
nor your lawyer.

The gardener's feet do no harm to the garden.

A wise man changes his mind, a fool never.

If you want to be revenged, hold your tongue.

Every potter praises his own pot and the more
if it be cracked.

A peasant between two lawyers
is like a fish between two cats.

Between saying and doing there is a long road.

Beads about the neck and the devil in his heart.

Half-way is twelve miles when you have fourteen miles to go.

He who has no shame has no conscience.

Suffer in order to know; toil in order to have.

A hundred years hence we shall all be bald.

Nothing is lost on a journey by stopping to pray
or to feed your horse.

Leave your jest while you are most pleased with it.

He is a good surgeon who has been well cut.

There's a Saying for That

All leaf and no fruit.

A woman's counsel is no great thing,
but he who does not take it is a fool.

Eaten bread is soon forgotten.

The foot of the owner is the best manure for his land.

Examine not the pedigree nor patrimony of a good man.

Great poverty is no fault or badness
but some inconvenience.

He who is not handsome at twenty, nor strong at thirty,
nor rich at forty, nor wise at fifty
will never be handsome, strong, rich nor wise.

Italy to be born in, France to live in, and Spain to die in.

A true word needs no oath.

Gossips fall out and tell each other truths.

A little loss frightens, a great one tames.

Love, grief and money cannot be kept secret.

The only remedy for love is—land between.

It is better to weep with wise men
than to laugh with fools.

It is good to have friends, even in hell.

The best mirror is an old friend.

He who denies all confesses all.

Desire beautifies what is ugly.

He who doubts nothing knows nothing.

He who has been stung by a scorpion
is afraid of its shadow.

A friend to everybody is a friend to nobody.

On the street of "by and by" one arrives at the house of
"never."

It is better to conceal one's knowledge
than to reveal one's ignorance.

He who is everybody's friend
is either very poor or very rich.

Do not rejoice at my grief, for when mine is old,
yours will be new.

Observe the face of the wife
to know the husband's character.

In a calm sea every man is a pilot.

A man who prides himself on his ancestry
is like the potato plant, the best part of which
is underground.

Bad news is always true.

When one will not, two cannot quarrel.

What belongs to everybody belongs to nobody.

Experience is not always the kindest of teachers,
but it is surely the best.

Poverty does not destroy virtue nor wealth bestow it.

We make more enemies by what we say
than friends by what we do.

Through not spending enough we spend too much.

He who has a good wife can bear any evil.

No woman sleeps so soundly that the twang of a guitar will
not bring her to the window.

Love is like a mousetrap; you go in when you want,
but you don't get out when you like.

God gives almonds to some who have no teeth.

There's a Saying for That

ITALY

Our religion and our language we suck in
with our milk.

A proverb is a child of experience.

Who would be loved must love.

A fool can ask more questions than seven wise men
can answer.

Great griefs are mute.

The heart does not think all the mouth says.

Our last garment is made without pockets.

If the patient dies, the doctor has killed him,
but if he gets well, the saints have saved him.

There's a Saying for That

A cask of wine works more miracles than a church full of saints.

No one knows less about his servants than their master.

He that never fails never grows rich.

He that seeks finds and sometimes what he would rather not

Who changes country changes luck.

Everything may be borne except good fortune.

The pen of the tongue should be dipped in the ink of the heart.

It is more easy to praise poverty than to bear it.

There are some who despise pride with greater pride.

That is pleasant to remember which was hard to endure.

He who knows the road can ride at full trot.

Try your friend with a falsehood and if he keep it a secret tell him the truth.

Nothing can come out of a sack but what is in it.

I satisfied, the world is satisfied.

It is better to do well than to say well.

"I-once-had" is a poor man.

The best throw upon the dice is never to play at them.

No man's head aches while he comforts another.

He who is an ass who takes himself to be a stag,
when he comes to leap the ditch finds his mistake.

Praise does a wise man good but a fool harm.

Even the sea, great as it is, grows calm.

Who would not have feet set on his neck,
let him not stoop.

A good servant makes a good master.

He that wants to beat a dog is sure to find a stick.

A sin confessed is half forgiven.

If I sleep, I sleep for myself; if I work, I know not for whom.

Every truth is not to be told.

When a tree is falling, everyone shouts, "Down with it!"

The example of good men is visible philosophy.

Not all are asleep that have their eyes shut.

Adam must have an Eve to blame for all his faults.

Men are as old as they feel and women as they look.

It is best to love wisely, no doubt, but to love foolishly
is better than not to love at all.

The sun passes over filth and is not defiled.

A man without a woman is a tree without leaves
and branches.

Girls dream of marriage; wives dream of love.

A bad agreement is better than a good lawsuit.

A silent passion increases more ardently.

Who has never done thinking
never begins doing.

A little truth makes the whole lie pass.

Silence was never written down.

No sooner is a law made than an evasion of it
is found out.

When love flees, it is futile to pursue it.

He that will have no trouble in this world
must not be born in it.

Either say nothing of the absent or speak like a friend.

He who blames grandees endangers his head,
and he who praises them must tell many a lie.

"I heard one say so" is half a lie.

A thousand probabilities do not make one truth.

Who offends writes on sand; who is offended, on marble.

He begins to grow bad who takes himself
to be a good man.

A burden which one chooses is not felt.

Suppers kill more than the greatest doctor ever cured.

Knowing is worth nothing unless we do
the good we know.

God save me from a bad neighbor
and from a beginner on the fiddle.

A man is half-known when you see him;
when you hear him speak you know him all out.

Learn wisdom by the folly of others.

Of money, wit and virtue, believe one fourth part of what
you hear men say.

Wise distrust is the parent of security.

He begins to grow bad who believes himself good.

Never spur a willing horse.

He who's about to speak evil of another, let him first well
consider himself.

One ill example spoils many good laws.

There's a Saying for That

The Italian is wise before he undertakes a thing,
the German while he is doing it
and the Frenchman when it is over.

In prosperity we need moderation; in adversity, patience.

There lies no appeal from the decision of Fortune.

Not to have been loved is a misfortune,
but not to have loved is a tragedy.

Lucky men need no counsel.

Three things only are done well in haste:
flying from the plague, escaping quarrels
and catching fleas.

'Tis better it should be said: "Here he ran away" than
"Here he was slain."

When gold speaks, every tongue is silent.

He who has good health is young, and he is rich
who owes nothing.

If young men had wit and old men strength enough,
everything might be well done.

One cannot hide love from a lover's eyes.

He who will have no judge but himself
condemns himself.

Everybody loves justice at another man's house;
nobody cares for it at his own.

That is a good misfortune which comes alone.

 There's a Saying for That

When the ship is sunk every man knows how she
might have been saved.

Old loves are never forgotten.

Affairs, like salt-fish,
ought to lie a good while soaking.

He who knows nothing is confident in everything.

Happy is the man who does all the good he talks of.

One pair of ears will drain dry a hundred tongues.

Love rules his kingdom without any laws.

A great deal of pride obscures, or blemishes,
a thousand good qualities.

He who is employed is tempted by one devil;
he who is idle by a hundred.

One father is sufficient to govern a hundred children;
a hundred children are not sufficient to govern one father.

He who speaks little needs half so much brains
as another man.

One who tries to unite prudence and love
knows nothing about love.

A civil answer to a rude speech costs not much,
and is worth a great deal.

There's a Saying for That

Speaking without thinking is shooting
without taking aim.

The first degree of folly is to think oneself wise;
the next to tell others so; the third to despise all counsel.

Men's years and their faults are always more than
they are willing to own.

Forgive every man's faults except your own.

Proverbs bear age, and he who would do well
may view himself in them as in a looking-glass.

Love perceives nothing as labor.

Hope is a pleasant kind of deceit.

A lewd bachelor makes a jealous husband.

A soldier, fire, and water soon make room
for themselves.

Have good luck and you may lie in bed.

The magic of the first love is the ignorance
that it can ever end.

If pride were a deadly disease, how many would
be now in their graves?

Begin your web and God will supply you with thread.

Time is a file that wears and makes no noise.

A wise man changes his mind
when there is reason for it.

There's a Saying for That

Old age is an evil desired by all men
and youth an advantage which no young man
understands.

That which seems probable is the greatest enemy
to the truth.

Virtue must be our trade and study,
not our chance.

Vices are learned without a teacher.

Live as they did of old, speak as men do now.

Break the legs of an evil custom.

Experience is the father and memory
the mother of wisdom.

Many know everything else
but nothing at all of themselves.

Six feet of earth make all men of one size.

He that is born of a hen must scrape for a living.

When children are little they make their parents'
heads ache; when they are grown up
they make their hearts ache.

Teeth placed before the tongue give good advice.

Little conscience and great diligence
make up your rich man.

Their power and their will are the measures princes
take of right and wrong.

True paradise is not in the heavens but upon the mouth
of a woman in love.

Go early to the market and as late as ever
you can to a battle.

Do not do evil to get good by it,
which never yet happened to any.

In the war of love, the one who flees wins.

Make a slow answer to a hasty question.

When one tries to hide love,
one gives the best evidence of its existence.

There's a Saying for That

THE MIDDLE EAST
TO CENTRAL ASIA

The ungrateful son is a wart on his father's face; to leave it is a
blemish, to cut it off is a pain.

Choose your neighbor before your house
and your companion before the road.

The wise man knows the fool, but the fool
does not know the wise man.

He is no wise man who authorizes another
to inflict injury.

Beware of one who flatters unduly; he will also
censure unjustly.

The world is like a dancing girl—
it dances for a little while to everyone.

The guest of the hospitable learns hospitality.

A wise man gets learning from those
who have none themselves.

A rich miser is poorer than a poor man.

During the pursuit of wisdom, man may be termed wise,
but the conceit of having attained it
renders him a fool.

Pretend not to that of which thou art ignorant,
lest thine actual knowledge be discredited.

Pardon is the choicest flower of victory.

Silence may be accompanied with one regret,
speech with many.

A little spark will set a whole city on fire.

Man learns little from success, but much from failure.

Truth may walk through the world unarmed.

A man profits more by the sight of an idiot
than by the orations of the learned.

He who forgives others, God forgives him.

To choose good is to avoid evil.

Words uttered are my masters, but words suppressed,
I am theirs.

Stand not before the king when he is in anger,
nor before a river when it is overflowing.

We are amply avenged on the envious man when we see him
dejected at our joy and happiness.

Who gives not thanks to men, gives not thanks to God.

Your secret is your prisoner; once you reveal it,
you are its prisoner.

Think of the going out before you enter.

Better a hundred enemies outside the house
than one inside.

Trust in God, but tie your camel.

If you buy cheap meat, when it boils you smell
what you have saved.

Three characteristics has a proverb: few words,
right sense, fine images.

The camel never sees its own hump, but that of its brother
is always before its eyes.

There's a Saying for That

Diligence is a great teacher.

One day honey, one day onion.

No man is a good physician who has never been sick.

 ARMENIA

The woman who loves her husband corrects his faults;
the man who loves his wife exaggerates them.

 KURDISTAN

If you cannot build a town, build a heart.

A wise man sits on the hole in his carpet.

With a sweet tongue and kindness,
you can drag an elephant by a hair.

A drowning man is not troubled by rain.

Doubt is the key of knowledge.

The most high god sees and bears; my neighbor knows
nothing, and yet is always finding fault.

A needle's eye is wide enough for two friends;
the whole world is too narrow for two foes.

A thoroughbred horse is not disgraced
by his bad saddle.

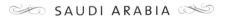 ## SAUDI ARABIA

Words from the heart reach the heart;
words from the mouth reach the ear.

 ## TURKEY

The devil tempts all other men, but idle men tempt the devil.

To beg of the miser is to dig a trench in the sea.

Experience is a precious gift, only given a man
when his hair is gone.

A weapon is an enemy even to its owner.

A cucumber being offered a fool,
he refused it because it was crooked.

A thousand friends are few; one foe many.

To a lazy man every day is a holiday.

Smoke does not make a pot boil.

No rose without a thorn nor love without a rival.

The only way to keep our thoughts is to fasten them in words
and chain them in writing.

Don't say amen to an unacceptable prayer.

Choose cloth by its edge, and a daughter by her mother.

A man does not seek his luck, luck seeks its man.

Two watermelons cannot be held under one arm.

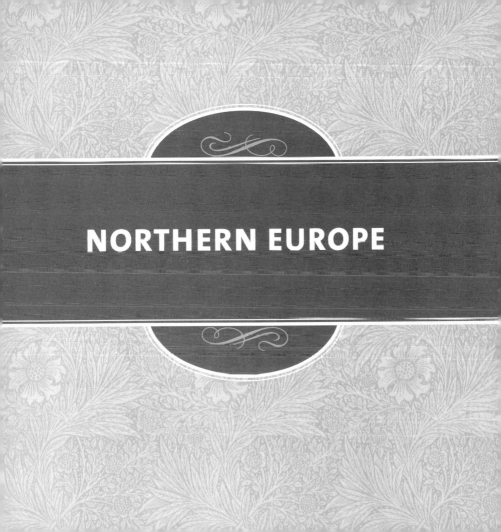

NORTHERN EUROPE

DENMARK

Faults are thick where love is thin.

He is young enough who has health, and he is rich enough who has no debts.

Nothing kills like doing nothing.

Everyone finds sin sweet and repentance bitter.

Rust consumes iron and envy consumes itself.

Gifts should be handed not hurled.

That which is unsaid may be said;
that which is said cannot be unsaid.

There's a Saying for That

Everyone rakes the fire under his own pot.

Speak little of your ill luck
and boast not of your good luck.

Love is one-eyed; hate is blind.

It is not all who turn their backs that flee.

A fool is like other men as long as he is silent.

There is no need to fasten a bell to a fool,
he is sure to tell his own tale.

Luck will carry a man across the brook
if he is not too lazy to leap.

It is no use hiding from a friend
what is known to an enemy.

Many a man is a good friend but a bad neighbor.

He who leaps high must take a long run.

Tell nothing to thy friend which thy enemy may not know.

If the beard were all, the goat might preach.

A rich child often sits in a poor mother's lap.

God gives every bird its food but does not thrust it
into its nest.

Jest with your equals.

One limps towards God, one leaps towards the devil.

Ten no's are better than one lie.

Peace feeds, war wastes; peace breeds, war consumes.

The poor man seeks for food,
the rich man for appetite.

 GERMANY

Love at first sight is the most common eye disease.

The old forget, the young don't know.

He who follows the crowd has many companions.

The eyes believe themselves, the ears other people.

A little too late is much too late.

Nothing weighs lighter than a promise.

In borrowing, an angel; in repaying, a devil.

Fear makes lions tame.

When one has seen the bear in the woods,
he hears his growl in every bush.

A fool who speaks the truth is better than
a hundred liars.

There is no one so rich that he does not still
want something.

A flatterer has water in one hand and fire in the other.

Even the lion must defend himself against the flies.

Many take by the bushel and give by the spoon.

Trust but not too much.

Repentance is the heart's medicine.

One peace is better than ten victories.

"We two have much to think about," said the louse
on the head of the philosopher.

Poverty is no shame, but being ashamed of it is.

Practice not your art, and 'twill soon depart.

If the prince wants an apple,
the servants take the tree.

A promised dollar is not worth half.

To question a wise man is the beginning of wisdom.

Revenge converts a little right into a great wrong.

Jealousy shuts one door and opens two instead.

A rich man without understanding
is a sheep with golden wool.

There's a Saying for That

There is no one so wise that wine
does not make him a fool.

Who will become rich must rise at four;
who is rich may lie till seven.

A hundred years of wrong do not make an hour of right.

God gives the wine but not the bottle.

Saving is a greater art than gaining.

Say not all thou knowest,
but believe all that thou sayest.

Better silent like a fool than talk like a fool.

A concealed spark is more to be feared
than an open fire.

Silence is as great an art as speech.

If I am seen I am joking; if I am not seen I steal.

The stomach is easier filled than the eye.

Petty thieves are hanged, people take off their hats
to great ones.

By three things we learn men: love, play and wine.

Time is anger's medicine.

A used plow shines; standing water stinks.

Forgive thyself nothing and others much.

He is lucky who forgets what cannot
be mended.

Luck gives many too much, but no one enough.

There is no one luckier than he
who thinks himself so.

When the fox wishes to catch geese
he wags his tail.

Two can lie the third to the gallows.

To give quickly is to give doubly.

God blesses the seeking, not the finding.

Silence is the answer to anger.

God is not hasty, but he forgets nothing.

A golden bit makes none the better horse.

Jealousy is the evil daughter of a good family.

The wise seek wisdom, the fool has found it.

God gives the milk but not the pail.

Where there is no jealousy there is no love.

There's a Saying for That

Truth has a handsome countenance
but torn garments.

He who has once burnt his mouth
always blows his soup.

Where God builds a church,
the devil builds a chapel.

There are many preachers who don't hear themselves.

Noble and common blood is of the same color.

When God says today, the devil says tomorrow.

East, west, home's best.

Unlooked-for comes oft.

He who is feared by many fears many.

Love grows with obstacles.

A good lie finds more believers
than a bad truth.

Praising is not loving.

The silent dog is the first to bite.

Jealousy is a pain which largely seeks
what causes pain.

A teacher is better than two books.

Nothing is so new as what has long been forgotten.

Friendship is a plant which one must water.

We give to the rich and take from the poor.

One has only to die to be praised.

The cats that drive the mice away are as good
as those that catch them.

The coffin is the brother of the cradle.

The first in the boat has the choice of oars.

Bear patiently what thou sufferest
by thine own fault.

Young fools think that the old are dotards,
but the old have forgotten more than the young fools know.

"Good day to you all," said the fox when he got
into the goose pen.

Who gives to me teaches me to give.

Where a man feels pain he lays his hand.

An ounce of patience is worth a pound of brains.

Shame lasts longer than poverty.

No one can have peace longer
than his neighbor pleases.

In the Land of Promise, a man may die of hunger.

No greater promisers than those
who have nothing to give.

Better poor on land than rich at sea.

Sickness comes on horseback and departs on foot.

Virtue consists in action.

Neither reprove nor flatter your wife
where anyone hears or sees it.

Patience surpasses learning.

Proverbs are the daughters of daily experience.

 SWEDEN

One should go invited to a friend in good fortune,
and uninvited in misfortune.

There's a Saying for That

RUSSIA

Distrust is the ax at the tree of love.

Pigs grunt about everything and nothing.

The cow that was eaten by the wolf
was the one that gave the most milk.

Not God but man makes pot and pan.

The darkness of night is more certain
than the light of the day.

We live in jest but die in earnest.

No priest's gown is so tight that the Devil
can't be buttoned up in it.

The lazy man hates even gold, if he has to drag it
out of the mountain.

Wild ducks and tomorrow both come without calling.

The thief is always afraid when the police cart
stops before his door.

Laziness is like the fastest greyhound, when it chases
the hare of excuse.

He feeds with the spoon, but pokes the eye
with the handle.
[trans. by Bob Blaisdell]

Death carries a fat tsar on his shoulders as easily
as a lean beggar.

Possessions bring worries;
poverty has them already.

The Devil is not so dangerous when he comes as a roaring
lion as when he comes as a wagging dog.

Where there's a trough, there'll be swine.

Thirst teaches best how valuable water is.

There is no heart so hard that the knife of temptation
cannot cut into it.

For a poor man even a wedding night is over too soon.
[trans. by Bob Blaisdell]

An enemy will agree, but a friend will argue.

When you live next to the cemetery,
you cannot weep for everyone.

If there's a back, there's a burden.

Every day learns from the one that went before,
but no day teaches the one that follows.

He that is afraid of bad luck will never know good.

When rubles fall from heaven there is no sack;
when there is a sack there are no rubles.

To run away is not glorious—but very healthy.

She loves the poor but can't stand beggars.
[trans. by Bob Blaisdell]

Happiness is not a horse—
you cannot harness it.

Law is a flag, and gold is the wind that makes it wave.

If you look for lasting peace, go to the cemetery.

Friendship is friendship, but business is business.
[trans. by Bob Blaisdell]

Wisdom is born, stupidity is learned.

Wine is poison for the young
and medicine for the old.

The devil can outwit a man; a woman can outwit ten.

The absent are always in the wrong.

Look after your clothes when they're spick and span,
and after your honor when you're a young man.

Paper won't blush, no matter what you write.
[trans. by Bob Blaisdell]

A word isn't a bird, if it flies out
you'll never catch it again.

He who weeps from his heart will provoke tears
even from the blind.

To deceive a deceiver is no deceit.

Every snipe praises its own bog.

Seven never wait for one.

That which is taken in with the milk only goes out
with the soul.

A kind word is pleasant, even to a cat.
[trans. by Bob Blaisdell]

Slow help is no help.

Some are wise and some are otherwise.

The straight cannot become straighter.

Don't boast when you set out,
but when you get there.

No need to scold when the fault is old.

Don't overwork a willing horse.

You can wipe out the sin, but not its memory.

Visiting is good; being home is better.

In each joke there's a drop of truth.
[trans. by Bob Blaisdell]

It never troubles a wolf how many sheep there are.

If you give a fool a knife,
you become a murderer.

The man who feeds his wife with vinegar
will suck no honey from her lips.

In a stranger's eye we see a piece of dust
but not the plank in our own.
[trans. by Bob Blaisdell]

Live a century, learn a century.

Live a century, learn a century, and die a fool!

If you're afraid of wolves, don't go in the woods.
[trans. by Bob Blaisdell]

Do not drink wine given to you; it will cost you more
than if you had bought it.

A fox sleeps but counts hens in his dreams.

There's a Saying for That

Truth is straight but judges are crooked.

Make thyself a sheep and the wolf is ready.

Every tribe has its thief, every mountain its wolf.

We may give advice, but we cannot give conduct.

Every vegetable has its season.

He that is deaf as a post is to be told
but once at most.

Throw nature out of the door, it will come back again
through the window.

Pretty merchandise sells more easily
than good merchandise.

Cowards talk most about war.

Repair your cart in December;
in July your sledge remember.

Allow him a finger and he'll bite off the whole arm.
[trans. by Bob Blaisdell]

Work is no bear, it won't go nowhere.

The shorter the parting the fewer the tears.

Water that stands still becomes poisonous.

The dog wags his tail at the food
rather than at his master.

Cruelty is the child of anger and revenge.

There's a Saying for That

Work done, have your fun.

Money likes to be counted.

Good news rests, but bad news runs.
[trans. by Bob Blaisdell]

Fools grow without watering.

A forgetful head makes a weary pair of heels.

A brief death ends the longest life.

If youth knew and age could.

True gold will shine through mud and slime.

Give every man thine ear, but few thy voice.

For the dead the immortality of fame; for the living
the immortality of love.

What's in the pocket just in case never seems
to take up space.

Teach a fool to bow his head to God,
he'll knock his block upon the floor.
[trans. by Bob Blaisdell]

A blind man falls less often than a seeing one.

The donkey may hide his ears, but his voice
will still betray him.

Grass grows without care, but not roses.

Laws rule people and gold rules laws.

There's a Saying for That

A word dropped from a song makes it all wrong.

Had I known where I would fall, I wouldn't
have come to that place at all.

No matter how much you feed the wolf,
he will still long for the forest.
[trans. by Bob Blaisdell]

What lures the fish is the worm, not the hook.

Too much butter won't spoil the porridge.

If one claw is caught, the bird is lost.

What's a game to the cat are tears to the mouse.

He that comes first to the hill may sit where he will.

Where goes the needle, there goes the thread.
[trans. by Bob Blaisdell]

The horse does not lift its tail without good reason.

You can't chop wood without making the chips fly.

Well begun is half done.

Seeing it once is better than hearing it a hundred.
[trans. by Bob Blaisdell]

Better late than never.

There's a Saying for That

The lame man hates the dancer.

One today is worth two tomorrow.

He who loves skiing downhill must enjoy
climbing uphill.

Love is not a potato that you can simply throw away.

Real love can't be smooth.

Brave against sheep, but a sheep
against the brave.

Velvet paws hide sharp claws.

There is small choice in rotten apples.

The truest jests sound worst in guilty ears.

None but a fool is always right.

Two in distress makes trouble less.

All are not saints that go to church.

Catch the bear before you sell his skin.

In the evening one may praise the day.

Books are often wiser than their readers.

When glory grows an inch,
pride grows a yard.

Be slow to promise and quick to perform.

He who makes no mistakes is he who does nothing.
[trans. by Bob Blaisdell]

There's a Saying for That

No man is a thief till he's caught.

Don't dig a hole for others or you will fall in it yourself.

The devil is not so terrible as he is painted.

Not enough salt is hardly a fault, but too much salt
is a cook's fault.

An uninvited guest is like a Mongol-Tatar invasion.

You cannot embrace the boundless.

Honey is sweet, but the bee stings.

Every man believes that God is his fellow countryman.

You must not blame the mirror for showing an ugly face.

Hunger breaks stone walls.

Speak well of the dead—or nothing at all.

One swallow does not make a summer.

If you're well off, don't seek better!

A little spark kindles a great fire.

The first pancake is always lumpy.

You cannot chop wood with a penknife.

There's a Saying for That

It's a poor soldier who doesn't hope to be a general.
[trans. by Bob Blaisdell]

Greet him according to his clothes,
take leave according to what he knows.

Repetition is the mother of learning.

There are mice under every roof.

No bees, no honey.

The law is a protection for the mighty
and a punishment for the peasant.

Truth has thorns.

Habit is second nature.

Truth is good, but happiness is better.

Mischiefs come by the pound and go away by the ounce.

Love doesn't mind a poor hut if there is a loving heart.

Hope is the fool's idol.

The shoemaker's wife is the worst shod.

Measure three times to cut once.
[trans. by Bob Blaisdell]

Words are not birds—out you let them,
and back you never get them!

Old love does not rust.

War is the worst disease.

An old friend is better than two who are new.
[trans. by Bob Blaisdell]

A man with a full belly thinks no one is hungry.

Labor and patience defeat all resistance.

The morn is wiser than the evening.

Better a wooden bed than a golden coffin.

Never offer to teach fish to swim.

Facts are a stubborn thing.

Enough is as good as a feast.

Better a bad peace than a good war.

Poverty is a sin that the rich cannot forgive.

No axe can cut out what a pen has written about.

The eye of the envious can see the cheese
but not the maggots.

The tongue ever turns to the aching tooth.

The chick doesn't teach the chicken.

What lies between a hammer and anvil
is soon knocked flat.

The wise man has long ears, big eyes and a short tongue.

There's a Saying for That

Together, testy; apart, bored.
[trans. by Bob Blaisdell]

Whether you boil snow or pound it,
you can only get water.

It is harder to lift the arm than the tongue.

Wine in, truth out.

Patience does not help always; impatience never does.

There's no knowing another's soul.
[trans. by Bob Blaisdell]

Almost doesn't count.

The apple doesn't fall far from the tree.

Better to ask the way than go astray.

My tongue is my enemy.

It is easier to pass laws than to obey them.

The chicken of love has often crawled
from the egg of pity.

The burden on the other man's shoulders
is always light.

Love does not look but sees everything.

There's a Saying for That

SOURCES

Hanan J. Ayalti. *Yiddish Proverbs.* Translated from the Yiddish by Isidore Goldstick. New York: Schocken Books. 1949.

Jonathan Clements. *The Little Book of Chinese Proverbs.* New York: Barnes and Noble Books. 2003.

Robert Christy. *Proverbs, Maxims, and Phrases of All Ages, Classified Subjectively and Arranged Alphabetically.* New York: G. P. Putnam's Sons. 1888.

(Editors at) Hippocrene Books. *Treasury of Love Proverbs from Many Lands.* New York: Hippocrene. 1998.

Rosalind Ferguson. *The Penguin Dictionary of Proverbs.* Second Edition. London: Markethouse Books. 2000.

Isabel Fonseca. *Bury Me Standing: The Gypsies and Their Journey.* New York: Knopf. 1995.

Patricia Houghton. *As Mad as a March Hare: The World of Proverbs.* Poole, Dorset: Javelin Books. 1981.

King James (translation). *The Bible.* 1611.

Tegwyn Jones. *A Little Book of Welsh Proverbs.* Belfast: Appletree Press. 1996.

Jan Knappert. *The A-Z of African Proverbs.* London: Karnak House. 1989.

S. S. Kuzmin and N. L. Shadrin. *Русско английский словарь пословиц и поговорок: Russian-English Dictionary of Proverbs and Sayings.* Moscow: Russky Yazyk Publishers. 1989.

David MacFarlane. *The Little Giant Encyclopedia of Proverbs.* New York: Sterling Publishing Company. 2001.

John Mapletoft. *Select Proverbs, Italian, Spanish, French, English, Scotish, British, &c., Chiefly Moral.* London. 1707.

Padraic O'Farrell. *Irish Proverbs and Sayings: Gems of Irish Wisdom.* Dublin: Mercier Press. 1980.

H. Pullar-Strecker. *Proverbs for Pleasure: Uncommon Sayings Collected, Arranged and Annotated.* New York: Philosophical Library. 1955.

John S. Rohsenow. *ABC Dictionary of Chinese Proverbs*. Honolulu, Hawai'i: University of Hawai'i Press. 2003.

Paul Rozenweig. *The Book of Proverbs: Maxims from East and West*. New York: Philosophical Library. 1965.

Jeff M. Sellers. *Folk Wisdom of Mexico*. San Francisco: Chronicle Books. 1994.

Christopher Shackle and Nicholas Awde. *Treasury of Indian Love: Poems and Proverbs from the Indian Sub-Continent*. New York: Hippocrene Books. 1999.

Jennifer Speake. *The Oxford Book of Proverbs*. Fifth edition. Oxford University Press. 2008.

Colin Walker. *Scottish Proverbs*. Edinburgh: Birlinn Limited. 2000.

Guy A. Zona. *Eyes That See Do Not Grow Old: The Proverbs of Mexico, Central and South America*. New York: Touchstone. 1996.

Guy A. Zona. *The Soul Would Have No Rainbow If the Eyes Had No Tears: And Other Native American Proverbs*. New York: Touchstone. 1994.